British Railway Diesel Memories

No. 63: 'D' for DIESELS : 4

David Dunn

INTRODUCTION

This, the fourth volume of D for Diesels will, in part, focus on some of the prototypes and ancestors of what were to become standard types of BR diesel locomotive. As usual, most of the illustrations contained herein have not been published previously so a feast of new and, in some cases, unusual material awaits the reader. The balance of main line and shunting types has been monitored, as has the selection of views of new factory fresh locomotives and those which have put in some service.

We are also going out onto the main line to look at various diesels in the landscape, working for a living rather than posing on shed. For those with an interest (which is all of you), we have a look at some more DBTs – Diesel Brake Tenders – those wonderful pieces of rolling stock which seemingly appeared from nowhere and then disappeared just as mysteriously. In a future volume we will take an even closer look at the origins, distribution and demise of those largely ignored but nevertheless fascinating vehicles.

With each volume so far published, we have presented a number of illustrations depicting diesel locomotives in trouble, one way or another, and we keep to that theme in this offering too.

So, sit back and enjoy the images herein. Who knows, you might spot a diesel near you.

Cover Picture
D6110 stables at Eastfield on Tuesday 6ᵗʰ August 1963. *D.J.Dippie.*

Title Page Picture
The London Midland Region appeared to like the 1-Co-Co-1 bogie arrangement of the trio of Bulleid/English Electric diesel-electrics and eventually ordered them in droves, albeit with a different body profile than that shown by 10203 and more in keeping with their own pioneer pair, 10000 and 10001. The Brighton-built 2,000 h.p. 'box' (Bulleid seemed to like his box designs) was captured on film departing Penrith with a Glasgow-Euston express on 23ʳᵈ June 1957. Note the chime whistle on the cab roof which was later replaced by twin air horns. Unlike sisters 10201 and 10202, this later example was not disfigured by the LMR addition of gangway doors for working in multiple. *R.H.Leslie.*

Printed and bound by The Amadeus Press, Cleckheaton, West Yorkshire
First published in the United Kingdom by Book Law Publications, 382 Carlton Hill, Nottingham, NG4 1JA

In reality the full height gangway doors retro-fitted to the Bulleid twins did not look too bad from this angle compared with some of those which were to be fitted on the Pilot-Scheme locomotives but close-up you could see they were not flush fitting. With 10202 leading, and complete with train headboard, the SR pair run south through Rockcliffe towards Carlisle with the southbound *ROYAL SCOT* on a glorious 1st December 1957. These two diesels were also fitted with chime whistles which they kept to withdrawal. Rated at 1,750 h.p., the SR pair, just like their LMS cousins, which were rated at 1,600 h.p., revealed the requirement that 2,000 h.p. or above was needed in a single unit if multiple working was to be avoided. *R.H.Leslie.*

Brand new 0-6-0DE No.13161 stands in the works yard at Darlington in August 1955 whilst a group of visitors admire its robust construction. Bound to spend all of its short life at Immingham shed, this was one of the Blackstone engined (non-standard) types which werc all withdrawn by April 1972, the bulk going in 1967. These non-standard '08s' were actually somewhat lighter than the English Electric engined versions (08 proper) and that variation differed more so depending on the type of traction motor fitted: the GEC version was some one-and-a-half tons lighter, whilst those equipped with the BTH traction motors (such as 13161 here) were two tons lighter. There was of course a further variation with Derby-built batch D3117 to D3126, which had Crossley engines and Crompton Parkinson nose suspended traction motors; all ten of those were allocated to Toton and were amongst the shortest lived of the 350 h.p. 0-6-0DEs, with four being withdrawn as early as December 1966. *R.F.Payne.*

D3243 at Heaton shed on 4th December 1960, a few months after being renumbered. Starting life at York in March 1956 as 13243, the 0-6-0DE transferred to Percy Main during the following June and then to Heaton in December 1958. Another Darlington built shunter, this one had an English Electric engine – standard – which basically ensured a longer life; twenty-two years in this case although it spent a third as much again awaiting a scrap yard to purchase it after withdrawal. *I.W.Coulson.*

Having no requirement of the essentials sort by steam locomotives – fire cleaning, water and continuous monitoring of the fire and boiler – diesel shunting locomotives could be left idling between duties or simply switched off and left for long periods unattended. Here at the erstwhile Dringhouses yard, just to the south of York on an unrecorded date but after May 1958, D3240 is stabled alongside residential property which, hopefully, perhaps was the abode of a railway enthusiast but probably wasn't. This shunter, as 08172, ended its career at Barrow Hill depot in August 1985, nearly attaining thirty years of operational service for BR. *J.W.Armstrong.*

A pair of Gateshead based locomotives – D3241 and D5111 trailing – make their way south for works attention on 16th April 1966. The shunter was en route to Doncaster whilst the Type 2 was going to Derby. In charge of the haulage is fellow stable mate D5182 and the trio is passing through Durham. The 0-6-0DE shunter has its coupling rods removed for the long distance transit. Note also how clean it appears compared with the normal Gateshead offering; that is easily explained by the fact that the shunter had just transferred from Percy Main on the closure of that north Tyneside depot. Full wasp stripes are painted on. How D5182 worked back home is unknown, nor even how far south it journeyed prior to returning. Normally any of these locomotives would have gone to Darlington for attention but that works had just closed its doors, forever! *A.Ives.* (*inset*) Some years earlier, whilst passing through Central station in Newcastle, D3241 displayed an early form of yellow warning panel/s on its rear end; apologies for not having an exact date for this image. *David Brown.*

(*above*) New Darlington-built 0-6-0DE shunters en route to their new homes! The unknown pair were seen heading south at York over the goods lines behind B16 No.61420 on an unrecorded date in the 1950s. (*below*) Another pair of Darlington new builds, albeit also unrecorded, seen at Doncaster this time behind a much more respectable B16, No.61422 in the 1950s. Note that the shunters, still in black livery, are travelling nose-to-nose for this delivery. There must have been some laid-down rules for these workings as both trains each have three open barrier wagons immediately behind the steam locomotive and then two further open wagons between the two diesel shunters, with the brake van coupled to the second diesel. The compiler would like to see further examples of these workings which have been recorded by readers. So, if you have any such images please contact the Publisher. Both *R.F.Payne*.

Gateshead depot had a long association with the 0-6-0DM shunters from the Drewry stable which became either TOPS Class 03 or 04. They were eminently suited to working Newcastle's Central station for a start and, in a perverse kind of way, kept alive a tradition, going back many decades, of having a small 0-6-0 shunting locomotive working at that place and being smartly turned-out too, as it was continuously in the public gaze; it is a shame the same could not be said for the main line locomotives from 52A. However, this was the Central station Pilot on an unrecorded date in 1962 with D2330 ticking over, awaiting the next lull in the main line workings before performing its next duty. From both private contractors and their own workshops, British Railways acquired nearly 400 of these useful locomotives between 1952 and 1962. They all had the same engine and mechanical parts and the only real difference, apart from the detail changes to their appearance over that decade of continuous construction, was in the size of their wheels. The earliest models had 3ft 3in. diameter wheels, changed to 3ft 6in. for the batches built from 1955, and finally, from 1957 a standard of 3ft 7in. was introduced. D2330 was built by Robert, Stephenson & Hawthorn and was put into traffic at Gateshead on 29th June 1961. A transfer to Percy Main on 28th May 1964 was hardly endorsed before it was returned to Gateshead on 14th July 1964. It was from 52A where it was withdrawn in July 1969, barely eight years old but a victim of extenuating circumstances. Like all the contractor-built examples this shunter became Class 04 whereas the BR-built shunters became Class 03, most of which survived for many years after the 04s were withdrawn. *B.Anderson.*

One of the 3ft 6in. wheeled versions of the Drewry diesel-mechanicals was D2242 which, as can be seen, was splendidly ex-works after a heavy overhaul in September 1962. The location of this scene is Northallerton and the little 0-6-0DM has called in to the low level yard by the engine shed whilst en route from Darlington back to its home shed at Neville Hill. Renumbered from 11212 in January 1959 during its last visit to the works at Darlington, this locomotive was one of those designated Class 04 under TOPS. New in October 1956, D2242 was withdrawn in October 1969 and later sold for scrap. It remained working from Neville Hill throughout its thirteen year career. *J.W.Armstrong.*

Hunslet 0-6-0DM D2576 of Thornton Junction shed was out-stationed to the one-road depot at Burntisland on Thursday 25th August 1966 and basks in the evening sunshine at that location. The diesel-mechanicals' duties included shunting the small wagon works located on the site of the former locomotive roundhouse. A pleasant job in the great scheme, not too taxing and with plenty of breaks in between movements – ideal. However, like many things which had a slow pace at that time, it was about to end and with redundancy came withdrawal. The nearby aluminium works would have been an ideal job for the likes of D2576 and its ilk but that place did not, apparently, require the use of a BR shunter because until about 1971 they had their own steam locomotives to handle interchange traffic. *J.W.Armstrong.*

Bowesfield Junction, 10th February 1968 with a Wickham-built d.m.u. on a Darlington–Middlesbrough service approaching a pair of busy diesel locomotives. Nearest is 0-6-0DE D3141, of Thornaby depot, which is shunting a pair of 16-ton mineral wagons loaded with scrap metals of various grades, no doubt generated by local engineering concerns. On the goods line is another locomotive from the Thornaby allocation, Clayton Type 1 D8602, which is on a working from Tees yard to ICI Billingham. The Bo-Bo had only arrived at 51L the day before having transferred from Gateshead, its home since entering traffic on 9th September 1964. The Claytons were ideal for the short trip working around industrial Teesside and Thornaby always had at least six 'on the books', and all from the same maker, Beyer, Peacock in Gorton. D8602 returned to Gateshead in May 1970, with both mechanical problems and the loss of suitable work being responsible for the concentration of the north-east area batch at 52A. On 26th April 1971, D8602 was sent to Haymarket where, along with some other still active members of the class, it remained until withdrawn later in the year. The overall feel of this scene is one of depression with the surrounding industrial building looking somewhat run-down, dilapidated, and derelict. Perhaps the view mirrored Britain's industrial fortunes which were at something of a low-ebb at this time in history and were never to recover. The overgrown siding leading off to the bottom left of the image once connected the factory where Metrovick Co-Bos were built but that too was now forlorn and abandoned, a decade having passed since the Co-Bos were first let loose onto BR. Ironically perhaps, the Metrovicks were, by 1968, into their last year of working, steam was coming to an end on BR and the country's finances were not exactly rosy. All in all, 1968 was not a vintage year. *John Boyes.*

D3182 shunts a long train of vans at Billingham alongside a plateau created from decades of tipping industrial waste. The date is given as 18th March 1968 but what appears to be a Peppercorn K1 2-6-0 steam locomotive at the head/tail of the ensemble brings that date into question. However, the date must be correct because D3182 did not arrive at Thornaby – from Bristol – until the penultimate day of 1967. On 20th April 1968 it was transferred to Polmadie, its brief four-month spell in Teesside completed. So, the date does fit nicely but what about that steam locomotive? This area of Teesside is still industrialised today with chemical plants providing plenty of business for the railway along the Seal Sands branch. D3182 had a fairly active life and after being delivered new from the works at Derby to St Philips Marsh shed on 15th October 1955, as 13182, it moved to nearby Bath Road shed on the eve of Bonfire Night 1961 – renumbering to D3182 had taken place six months beforehand – but went to Marsh Junction depot on 28th November 1964. After its re-allocation to Polmadie in 1968, it then moved between various depots in Scotland and became 08116 in March 1974. Returning to England, the 0-6-0DE ended up at Gateshead from where it was withdrawn in August 1982. (*inset*) The presence of the steam locomotive is explained by Peppercorn K1 No.62005 being used by the ICI North Tees works at Port Clarence to raise steam. Just prior to Christmas 1967 the ICI plant had suffered a breakdown within its steam raising plant. Shortly after the Christmas break 62005 was towed to the rescue (it had been withdrawn 30th December and was stored at Neville Hill) and for six weeks provided the necessary for the works. A fireman from West Hartlepool was provided, along with tankers carrying pure water; use of the latter got rid of the need to wash out the boiler. Coal was also taken in by road. This was the smoky scene on 28th February 1968. Both *John Boyes.*

Another new-build on delivery! D3879, ex-Crewe, was captured on film at Kingmoor shed on Saturday 14th May 1960, whilst en route to St Margarets shed. Ex-shops on 28th April, the 0-6-0DE had undergone a number of tests prior to being released to traffic but it still had to complete its delivery run before earning any revenue. Part of a batch of sixteen – being supplied to 64A between April and June 1960 – D3879 looks resplendent in green livery with the, by now, standard wasp stripes. Note the twin handles on the cab door, another innovation copied from the private contractors and added to the BR design. *D.J.Dippie.*

Remember D2410 in Vol.2? Well here it is working its home turf at Inverness Rose Street on an earlier date, believed to be circa 1960. Comparison of the two images show the little diesel has sans wasp-stripes in this view and that the BR crest is located on the second panel from the front of the bonnet; that position probably changed every time the 0-4-0DM had the panels removed for shed maintenance because the crest fitted nicely onto a single panel width. Note also that the styles of the fleet numbers – Tri-ang or Palitoy? – are the same as depicted in the July 1963 image although in this illustration they appear to be closer together. *J.W.Armstrong*.

Here is a nice enough scene. Staying north of the border, we have NBL 0-4-0DH No.11707 performing on a trip working through Falkirk Grahamston, and heading back to Polmont at midday on Saturday 6th July 1957, at a steady 12 m.p.h., its maximum speed! The little shunter had been a resident of Polmont shed since the previous October but on 2nd November 1957, it transferred back to Dunfermline from whence it arrived. Renumbered D2707 on 14th February 1959 during overhaul at Cowlairs, the four-coupled diesel performed from 62C for a further ten years before withdrawal. Beyond the bridge is the former North British Railway passenger station with the Grahamston name which opened in 1850 simply as Falkirk. It became Falkirk Grahamston in 1903 and is still open for business. Two other passenger stations still exist in Falkirk, High on the direct line to Glasgow (Queen Street), and Camelon about a mile west of this location. *C.J.B.Sanderson.*

One of Thornaby's BRC&W Type 2 Bo-Bos, D5374, makes use of the avoiding lines at Newcastle Central station to deliver a failed Derby Lightweight d.m.u. to Heaton depot on a rather damp day in 1964. The Thornaby batch, which fell into the number range D5370 to D5378, was delivered new to that depot between 17th January and 7th March 1962. However, in January 1966 they were all re-allocated to the Midland Lines of the London Midland Region. Eventually of course all of those LMR examples found their way to the Scottish Region and became TOPS Class 27. *B.Anderson.*

A nice three-quarter view of D5308 at the head of a King's Cross train in Cambridge station on Monday 11th May 1959. Relatively new at this time – delivered to Hornsey during the previous December – the Type 2 still has a fairly clean and glossy finish to its paintwork. Although most of the twenty examples of BRC&W Type 2s initially allocated to the GN main line went to Finsbury Park depot when it opened for business on 24th April 1960, this particular locomotive was not amongst them. It had been transferred to Haymarket on that same day, along with D5302, D5303 and D5307. *I.W.Coulson.*

It was said that the steam-diesel combination at engine sheds did not improve the appearance of the latter but that fact was brought into question shortly after the end of steam on various regions at different times. By 1st December 1968 steam had been banished from BR for nearly four months but many of the diesels still remained filthy as witness this 'Deltic' passing through Backworth station on that winter Sunday. The extremely grotty looking D9014 THE DUKE OF WELLINGTON'S REGIMENT of Gateshead (shades of the A4s external condition here – was it a 52A tradition that their top link locomotives should be presented in ever worsening states?) is at the head of a diverted London (King's Cross)–Edinburgh (Waverley) express. In order to bypass weekend engineering work on the ECML, this train would probably have been subjected to numerous speed restrictions during its passage through the heart of the Northumberland coalfield which was, even then, still very active. Perhaps D9014 was in fact wearing 'camouflage' to blend in with the local motive power. Replacing an earlier passenger station located a little to the north and east on the Blyth & Tyne line, the station here was opened by the North Eastern Railway in June 1864. Originally named Hotspur, it was quickly renamed Backworth, and passed into history when it closed on 13th June 1977 but the route is still available for diversions. *John Boyes.*

Besides the locomotives being painted at the front end with yellow warning panels, it became the practice to paint the ends of the diesel brake tenders (DBTs) propelled by the locomotives. This is Gateshead EE Type 3 D6795 propelling an unidentified DBT through the seemingly rural landscape of Shincliffe, County Durham, on 8th December 1968 – winter haze has restricted the vision somewhat and blocked out any colliery headgear which might otherwise have been in view – en route to a Sunday mineral working; it was, after all, winter. Note the shunters pole now has its own brackets fixed on the front of the DBT, continuing an age old North Eastern practice of locating such poles at the front of the motive power whilst travelling between yards. *John Boyes.*

Over the years of transition from steam to diesel traction (and beforehand too), the iron ore trains plying between Tyne Dock and Consett have seen many different types of locomotives attached to the head, and tail, of these workings. In this undated view from the spring of 1965, at Annfield East, EE Type 4 D393 of Gateshead gives a helping push to the BR 9F 2-10-0 which is heading a loaded train towards the steel works at Consett. It was normal for the banking engines to wait on a spur at South Pelaw junction for the westbound trains, and buffer up without the train stopping. After their laborious task was completed, they dropped off at Medomsley. Although weighing-in at less than 1000 tons, and consisting eight or nine hoppers, these formations travelled over one of the steepest inclined routes on British Railways, hence the top-and-tail combination requirement for much of the journey. Eventually the BR Sulzer Type 2 Bo-Bos (Class 24 version) found regular employment with these workings whilst the Type 4s were used as both train engine and banking power during the interim until the Type 2s took up the reigns permanently. *B.Anderson.*

En route to Consett, this iron ore train from Tyne Dock is now in the hands of a pair of BR Sulzer Type 2s which became the preferred motive power shortly after steam was eventually withdrawn from the workings at the end of the summer timetable in 1966. To enable the Type 2s to take over the trains, they had to be modified at Crewe whereby extra air equipment was fitted which then enabled them to open and close, and keep closed, the hopper wagon doors. Photographed passing Low Fell – the route here is quite easy and the hard work started after branching off the main line at Ouston junction – D5107 leads D5102 at some period during the summer of 1968. Altogether ten of the class (D5102 to D5111 all of Gateshead) were modified for these duties; exactly the same number as the 9F 2-10-0 steam locomotives formerly based at Tyne Dock shed. Once fully deployed, the pair of Bo-Bos, working in either tandem or multiple, did not require banking assistance over any section of the route. Note that D5107 is now sporting the BR double-arrow logo, and on both cabs; D5102 retains the BR crest introduced in 1957. Though starting their careers at Gateshead some three months apart in 1960, both locomotives ended up in Scotland as 24107 and 24102 and were withdrawn in 1976 at Haymarket and Inverness respectively. *Trevor Ermel.*

What to do when the train indicating blind packs-in – improvise – as has been done by whichever depot was responsible for releasing Brush D1846 to work this southbound express recorded at Preston in 1968. At this time the Crewe-built Co-Co was allocated to the LMR's Western Lines and was already three years old having been initially allocated to the diesel depot at Crewe when put into traffic on 29th May 1965. Along with many of the LM diesel locomotive fleet, D1846 was soon to become part of the newly formed D05 Stoke Division (17th June 1968) as the LMR yet again re-organised its motive power disposition (such paper transactions might have kept a number of BR personnel employed over the years but it played havoc with the ABC shed books). However, it did help to speed up the elimination the cast-iron shed plates from the motive power scene although it was 1973 before a revised code and an alternative display method was introduced. Meanwhile, for those who have yet to spot any form of allocation on this Brush, the 'W' is just below the number, above the worksplate. The apparent straight horizon of the illustration is actually a parcels bridge which had recently been erected at Preston station. *Trevor Ermel.*

(*above*) On Saturday 14th May 1960, Carlisle Upperby engine shed yard hosted three of the original 'Peaks' in the form of D4, D5, and D6, along with a rather dirty EE Type 4 which was D216. This scene was recorded shortly after the ten Derby-built Type 4s had been transferred to the WCML to evaluate their performance in comparison with the EE Type 4s. Of the trio, D4 was allocated to Camden on this date whilst D5 and D6 were Upperby residents, along with D216. (*opposite, top*) D4 GREAT GABLE appears bereft of any shed plates but it had only arrived at Camden four weeks prior to this scene being recorded on film; nine of the ten initially went to 1B and most were dispersed to other WCML sheds soon thereafter, so a reluctance on behalf of Camden to fit shed plates was understandable. However, with this particular 'Peak' they did eventually fit some and it remained at 1B until called to Toton and a lifetime of freight workings on 17th March 1962. (*opposite, bottom*) Upperby must have had the same ideas regarding shed plates because they too have failed to fit any to D5 CROSS FELL or D6 WHERNSIDE. The former did in fact transfer back to Camden on 16th July whereas the latter remained at 12B until 3rd March 1962 when it too was re-allocated to Toton. This closer view of D6 shows a rather dirty locomotive which had been recently haphazardly 'cleaned'. All *D.J.Dippie*.

(*opposite*) Contemporary records show that EE Type 3s D6735 and D6736 were both allocated, when new, to Hull Dairycoates, the precise recorded dates being Tuesday 17th April 1962 and Wednesday 25th April 1962 respectively. However, these illustrations captured on film on Friday 4th May 1962, show that the pair were actually at Thornaby shed, D6735 having a 51L shedplate already fixed beneath its fleet number at the No.1 end! Mystery? It appears so because both locomotives have that new look about them. Even the buffer heads seem hardly touched. So, what was happening? One theory is that the pair had been sent together to 51L rather than 50B by mistake; a situation which, if not unique, was certainly rare. How long the pair resided at Thornaby is unknown. More than likely they had been sent 'on loan' for the Thornaby crews to 'get a feel of them' prior to the arrival of the first allocated examples (D6755 to D6778) during the following September. The shedplate has really thrown the spanner in the works however because it was not usual to fit such an item for a loan period. It was a strange time on BR during those days of transition. (*above*) With Tees yard in the distance, the errant Type 3s stable at the east end of Thornaby shed yard alongside their larger Type 4 cousins – D247 and D251, both of Gateshead – trying, perhaps, to blend in. The drainage suction pump has got its cap and coat on, so it must be going home time! All *D.J.Dippie*.

Another new English Electric product newly arrived on BR property was Type 4 D234 which is stabled in the Paint shop yard at Doncaster on Sunday 27th September 1959 after its Friday journey from Vulcan Foundry. Destined for the London Midland Region, initially Crewe and then to Edge Hill on 31st October 1959, the biggest locomotive on the yard has one of those pathetic little ladders fitted which were to disappear long before all of the class were delivered. It's worth keeping an eye out for further examples within this and other albums in the series. As mentioned before, these locomotives were supplied as an interim measure on the LMR because by 3rd January 1965 this particular locomotive was transferred from Liverpool to Rugby to help haul the WCML expresses over the final un-electrified section of the route into Euston. Thereafter, D234 was relegated, along with the rest of the LMR contingent, to secondary passenger work and freight status. Behind is BRC&W Type 2 newcomer D5312, along with one of the more usual habitants represented by Thompson A2 No.60504 nearer the shop. *I.H.B.Lewis.*

D207, from the initial batch of ten, is whistling away in platform 8 at Newcastle (Central) at the head of an Up express in late September 1958. This particular Type 4 was allocated to Hornsey in July 1958 and like the other examples working on the GN main line moved to the new purpose-built depot at Finsbury Park on 24th April 1960. In June 1961, D207 transferred to the GE lines working from Stratford depot and was soon joined by the others of the '1st 10' so that for the first time all of the Pilot Scheme EE Type 4s were working in the same area. In April 1966, all ten moved again but to Ipswich for a final fling on the GE lines prior to their inter-regional transfer to the LMR. D207 went to the non-descript Western Lines allocation on 2nd September 1967 but was not based at any particular depot until 6th April 1968 when it transferred to Allerton. Eventually the majority of the EE Type 4s ended their days working from just a handful of depots which included Healey Mills, Kingmoor, Longsight, Springs Branch, Thornaby and York. D207, as 40007 worked finally from Healey Mills depot and was withdrawn in February 1983. Not a bad innings for an 'interim measure'. Note the brazier merrily burning in the '6ft' with a little supply of coal lay on the ground between the sleepers; no doubt an early season anti-frost measure for the overhead water cranes. What would H&S think of that little trick nowadays – evacuate the station prior to the conflagration, close the ECML between Darlington and Berwick. It would no doubt be a measure designed to annoy, delay and frustrate as many people as possible! *H.Forster.*

Although St Margarets shed had no main line diesels allocated, it certainly entertained a fair number of 'foreign' and Haymarket based locomotives. This is one of the former, EE Type 4 D396 from Gateshead – where else – on Friday 9th August 1963. Even now, at just over a year old, the big 1-Co-Co-1 had been relegated to working secondary passenger services and mixed traffic duties. Within four years D396 would be transferred to Healey Mills where, for the rest of its life, it would be working mainly freight traffic. Its final depot was Longsight where the 2000 h.p. leviathans were appreciated perhaps a little bit more. It finally bowed out in May 1984 and was eventually hauled to Doncaster where its acceptance had been carried out during the summer of 1962. However, this time Doncaster became its final resting place. *D.J.Dippie.*

Yet another 'foreigner' at St Margarets on that August Friday in 1963 and from – you've guessed it – Gateshead. Derby-built Sulzer Type 4 D182, which was less than a year old, 'graced' the shed yard after working in to Edinburgh with 5N00. This is one of the 'Peaks' which became Class 46 (D138 to D193) on account of it having different traction motors (Brush) than the majority of the class (D11 to D137) which had Crompton-Parkinson motors. Approximately half of the locomotives which became Class 46 were initially allocated to 52A but by the time of their withdrawal period – 1978 to 1984 – most of them were resident at Gateshead. The eight or so which did not end their days at 52A were allocated to Plymouth Laira at the time of their demise. *D.J.Dippie.*

Shortly after its arrival on the Great Northern main line, D206 was photographed passing through Hornsey with a lightweight Up morning express in July 1958. Judging by the number of vehicles, and the Buffet cars inside the formation, it was probably one of the *CAMBRIDGE BUFFET CAR EXPRESS* trains which plied their trade between Cambridge and King's Cross numerous times throughout the day. *H.Forster.*

The Stockton works of Metropolitan-Vickers was the birthplace of one of British Railways worst nightmares – the Co-Bo Type 2! Note the edge of the turntable pit on the left. Not a lot of people realised that the locomotive manufacturers had to invest in such equipment in order to stay competitive – I wonder what diameter it was? D5701 is the supposed subject of the illustration and in this Sunday 31st August 1958 view the pristine locomotive appears somewhat reluctant to leave the security and safety of the pastures of scrubland surrounding the Stockton factory. I wonder why! It must be admitted though that the paint finish was nice. *H.Forster.*

Brush D5538 was a new arrival at Doncaster by the 5th July 1959 (actual arrival Thursday 2nd July). In Vol.1 we touched on the delivery routes followed, and procedures undertaken, by these Loughborough built locomotives which, up to the time of this latest arrival, were mainly undertaken singularly with only a few pairs arriving at Doncaster at the rate of once a month. However, after production had been stepped-up at the end of that summer, Brush began sending out the new locomotives at the rate of two every week from D5558 and D5559 onwards (22nd October 1959) and coupled together too. *H.Forster.*

(*above*) Also in the works yard on that 5th July 1959 was BRC&W Type 2 D5332 en route to Scottish Region, acceptance permitting, with the recess for the tablet-catching equipment prominent. We keep looking at the position of the door handles on these locomotives and this one has them in the lower third of the door panel. It is worth noting the finish of the paintwork with these new deliveries – just look at the Type 4s bodywork reflecting D5332's number as though a mirror. (*below*) Five weeks earlier, on 31st May, D5326 was present and this illustration shows the opposite No.2 end. Note that EE Type D242 in the rear has a little ladder. Both *H.Forster.*

A nice virtually uncluttered view of the Paint shop yard at Doncaster with two EE Type 4s in residence on an unrecorded Sunday but at sometime in late May 1961. With D346 nearest and D345 beyond, Vulcan Foundry had apparently released them a week apart – 24th and 17th May respectively – according to 'official' figures but they appear to be an item and may well have arrived from Newton-le-Willows together. What was certain is the fact that both locomotives were bound for Neville Hill shed once their acceptance was completed. Note the complete absence of any warning panels at this early date. *K.Linford*.

Brush Type 2 D5835 double-heads a southbound express – or holiday extra – through York Holgate with a Thompson B1 as train engine. Clean diesel, dirty steam locomotive; a not uncommon combination at the time (admittedly unrecorded) but study the front end of the Brush. Has anyone an idea as to what that is? First thought was a very elaborate train headboard carrier/bracket which seems the only logical answer. My second thought was a bicycle carrier such as those which have recently been adorning private motor vehicles – and we know how railwaymen in the 1960s enjoyed their own two-wheel transport. Who knows? Perhaps an inventive footplateman has left his cycle in Scarborough or the headboard has fallen off. Answers on a bike please to...! *K.Linford.*

(*opposite*) DP1, or simply DELTIC to it's friends. In these 9th September 1956 illustrations, the big blue locomotive and its support coach are found sheltering inside the repair shop at Kingmoor motive power depot. By now DELTIC had spent nearly a year on the London Midland Region having been on loan for evaluation which entailed numerous trials and even more work hauling WCML expresses, especially those between Euston and Liverpool. During that time DELTIC was allocated to Speke Junction engine shed but it could be summoned to work anywhere hence the requirement for a support coach to carry all the necessary specialist tools and equipment to keep it running whenever it wandered away from 8C. Externally the Co-Co appears to looking its best and no doubt the English Electric Co. had some input regarding the cleaning and appearance of the locomotive whilst it was with BR. Designated DP1, that appellation was never carried and instead only the name of the installed engines or prime movers, were ever displayed. DP2 on the other hand carried that designation but no name; in reality even the DP2 was technically incorrect because 'Deltic' engines were not employed as the prime mover on that locomotive although, it looked like a 'Deltic' that's for sure. *F.W.Hampson.*

(*below*) Whilst a white boiler-suited EE engineer looks on, what looks like a steam man peers into the noisy innards of DELTIC at Crewe on an unrecorded summertime date in the late 1950s when it was in charge of a Down WCML express. Did anybody ever see that huge headlight working, or was it just for show? *C.J.B.Sanderson.*

Another view of DELTIC, and its train at Crewe from a different angle; impressive or what? Not according to the LMR authorities, or did they have their minds on other things? *C.J.B.Sanderson.*

On moving to the Eastern Region, DELTIC must have really impressed the right people at King's Cross because eventually an order for twenty-two production models materialised. In April 1960 the big demonstrator was not looking its best externally when photographed in the rather cramped confines of the 'Bottom Shed' locomotive yard at King's Cross station. By now it was allocated to Hornsey, its final BR home. It was eventually allowed to retire in March 1961 when the first three of the '22' had been delivered for acceptance trials at Doncaster. *D.J.Dippie.*

A final look at DELTIC on the ECML. Wherever it went the big noisy blue diesel got an audience. This is Grantham in 1960 with a southbound express about to depart. The people working on and those living near the ECML were soon to endure twenty-odd years of these noisy beasts, day in, day out! *A.R.Thompson* collection.

Every inch a 'Deltic' – not quite! Those two inset ventilator grills for a start had nothing to do with DP1 nor any of the production batch but otherwise, DP2 did look the part. On 1st June 1966 the Class 50 prototype was heading south along the ECML near Burnmouth with what looks like the *ANGLO-SCOTTISH CAR CARRIER*. This 'demonstrator' had been working BR metals for some four years by this time, initially on the LMR but most of that time had been on the ECML based at Finsbury Park. Ironically, it was the Region on which it spent the least time which ordered its ilk; initially on a lease basis from the manufacturer because BR was broken financially. *C.J.B.Sanderson.*

An undated photograph, probably January 1962, of the first 'Western' D1000 WESTERN ENTERPRISE, outside Swindon shops with other diesel-hydraulics for company. This may possibly date from the time when D1000 was new and undergoing prolonged road testing hence the 'just in traffic' appearance; the Z in the headcode indicates that some kind of test train had been hauled recently. The Hymek in the left background looks fairly new and those had been delivered up to about D7015 by the time D1000 was turned out, and up to D7023 when D1000 eventually went into traffic. However, the final two digits of the B-B's number are hidden so we cannot be sure. The 'Warship' behind was well weathered but most of them had been around for a couple of years by this time so no clues there either. *I.S.Jones.*

Remember the illustration in Volume 3 of EE Type 1 D8085 in something of a mess at St Rollox engine shed in October 1961? Well here it is again, some three years later and working a Down freight through Thornhill on the Sou-West' main line looking none the worse for its ordeal but its once pristine paint finish is by now obliterated by filth. You might also remember that it was one of the pair chosen (D8086 being the other) to be fitted with special air brake equipment and connections which enabled them to haul empty electric multiple units over non-electrified routes between depots. The external components of that special air brake are clearly visible in this rather damp August 1964 view. Note the Polmadie 66A shed code painted on the bufferbeam between the two air lines; yet another example of detail regarding the diesel fleet and the way depots approached the application of such detail with different locomotives. A frontal picture of D8086 with the new brake equipment also appeared in Vol.3. *A.Vitty.*

Is that the old Hornby-Dublo model before us? No, it's D8004 looking every bit the part though. Standing at Willesden Junction on 14th August 1957, the recently delivered Type 1 (it appears to have just arrived, and seemingly hauled down 'dead' from Vulcan Foundry because there is no soot around the exhaust ports) was to undergo acceptance trials from Willesden engine shed prior to undertaking its official allocation to Devons Road diesel depot on 24th August. What about that roof then? *H.Forster.*

Continuing the BRC&W Type 2 door handle saga, we present D5310 stabled at Carlisle Canal shed on Sunday 25th February 1962. Now well and truly a part of the Scottish Region diesel fleet, D5310 shows the minor detail and subtle differences which came about with the class after D5300 was first accepted by British Railways. D5300 had no serifs on the 'D' prefix whereas this example on D5310 clearly has; the bottom line of the number group was initially placed in line with the bottom of the central band wrapped around the body but D5310 has it's number located so that the band is central to the number position. The lamps irons, or brackets, on D5300 to D5305 were situated so that they protruded into the line of the said white band and, were further in from the corner of the cab, basically in line with the electric lights; they remained like that on those early members of the class until well into TOPS days. D5310 had them just on the corner and positioned below the electric lights. Note that our subject is not fitted with any shed plates even though the fixing screws are in place. Another bit of detail in view, totally unrelated but nevertheless interesting, is the buffer stop which, it will be noted, is formed of three horizontal rails, three vertical rails, and three angled rails, all joined together with chunky fillet plates. *George Watson.*

Not quite a 'contra-flow' but enough 'traffic cones' around to suit any 0-6-0DM fan. This is Kings Lynn diesel depot on the penultimate day of February 1960 with only D2010 identified. However, at this time seven of these locomotives were allocated to 31C and six of them are on view here. So which one was missing? The choice is yours from D2011, D2012, D2013, D2014, D2015, and D2030. The first and last mentioned were relative newcomers to the shed having arrived during the previous week ending 20th February. The other five were, by now, quite old hands and had been resident at Kings Lynn since 28th March 1958 (2011, 2012), and 16th May 1958 (2013, 2014, 2015) respectively. On 29th September 1960, all seven were transferred to March depot but remained working from this place which eventually became a stabling point albeit with a purpose-built one-road refuelling and servicing shed. The old steam shed was demolished (photographic evidence of that event reveals a steam locomotive being employed to 'haul' down the walls with the aid of a wire strop) and the place became home for some half dozen main line locomotives and an equal number of shunters. The 31C coding was lost in July 1962. *H.Forster.*

The LNER-built engine shed at Norwich City was closed by British Railways on 25th February 1959 but in the illustration captured on a winter Saturday, one year and two days later, it was still very much in use and housing Drewry 0-6-0DM D2037 (itself only a year old) which was out-stationed from Norwich Thorpe depot. The shed was erected in 1942 as a result of the previous engine shed being destroyed, a victim of a German bombing raid in 1941. The corrugated iron shed – what else – with its girder frame was much luckier than its predecessor and now resides on one to the preserved railway sites in the area. D2037, withdrawn from Norwich in September 1976, as 03037, was sold off to industry and initially went to work at the Oxcroft coal disposal point near Chesterfield, which was quite a change of scenery from Norfolk. *H.Forster.*

One of the vacuum fitted – for train braking – members of the contractor-built Drewry class, 11217 became D2247 on 10th March 1959 whilst being overhauled at Darlington. However, on 16th February 1957, when just a few months old, the 0-6-0DM was caught on camera at Heaton shed stabled next to the depot's breakdown train. At this time the shunter was actually allocated to Percy Main; most of the north Tyneside area shunters were in fact allocated to 52E, which had been adapted for their maintenance requirements. Joining the Percy Main allocation on 14th December 1956, 11217 transferred to North Blyth in time for Christmas 1958. Gateshead acquired it on 8th June 1963 but a year later it cut its links with the north-east and moved south to Neville Hill. Finally, in December 1968 it was transferred to York where it remained until withdrawn just eleven months later. Note the large tank behind the front end steps (see also D2242) which was also duplicated on the right side of the shunter in the same position. The positioning of the tanks restricted the size of the shunters' step at the front end and required the shunter to hold and hang on rather than stand on a platform as was the case with the more generous 03s. *H.Forster.*

This Vulcan Foundry-built Drewry 0-6-0DM was one of the 3ft 3in. diameter wheeled examples but as luck would have it, we cannot see to compare the smaller wheels with other 04s. Instead we are presented with one of the skirt-fitted examples, No.11103 which became D2203 in October 1958 at Stratford. Skirting or side rod protection plating as it was also known, and fore-and-aft 'cow-catchers' became a Board of Trade requirement many decades previously for any shunting locomotive working over public roads; and you thought the H&SE were fussy. For the record Nos.11100 to 11103 were fitted with the side skirting. The date of this photograph is 11th May 1958, a Sunday, and the six-year old locomotive has already got the fairly new BR crest adorning its cab side from a recent visit to Stratford works for overhaul. The location is Yarmouth Vauxhall engine shed during its final year of operation as a working depot. Note the chimney which is simply a pipe, simple, austere, adequate. Also, this locomotive was fitted with vacuum brakes for carriage shunting. *W.R.E.Lewis.*

Here, for comparison, is another one of the fifteen early Drewry shunters fitted with 3ft 3in. wheels. D2204 is on the shed yard at Darlington on Sunday 15th March 1959 with a WD Austerity 0-6-0 saddletank (J94) for company. New to West Hartlepool shed on 6th March 1953 as No.11105, this six-coupled shunter transferred to Thornaby on 2nd September 1967 but two weeks later it was resident at Bradford's Hammerton Street depot where it worked out its remaining days on BR prior to withdrawal in October 1969. Again the simple pipe chimney/exhaust is employed, this one with a subtle rim fitted. These early shunters were equipped with whistles (at the top of the cab front plate) rather than air horns but some were later fitted with horns, especially those on 'street duty'. Vacuum for train braking appears to have been fitted to all of these first fifteen locomotives. The ladders and the box on top of the bonnet appear to be fairly new fittings; 11105 certainly did not enter traffic when new with such 'embellishments' but it did have them before renumbering took place (see next). Note that the 0-6-0DM has a wrong facing crest at this period; probably applied when the locomotive was renumbered in May 1958. A small 'D' which was sans serifs is employed over green livery. *N.W.Skinner.*

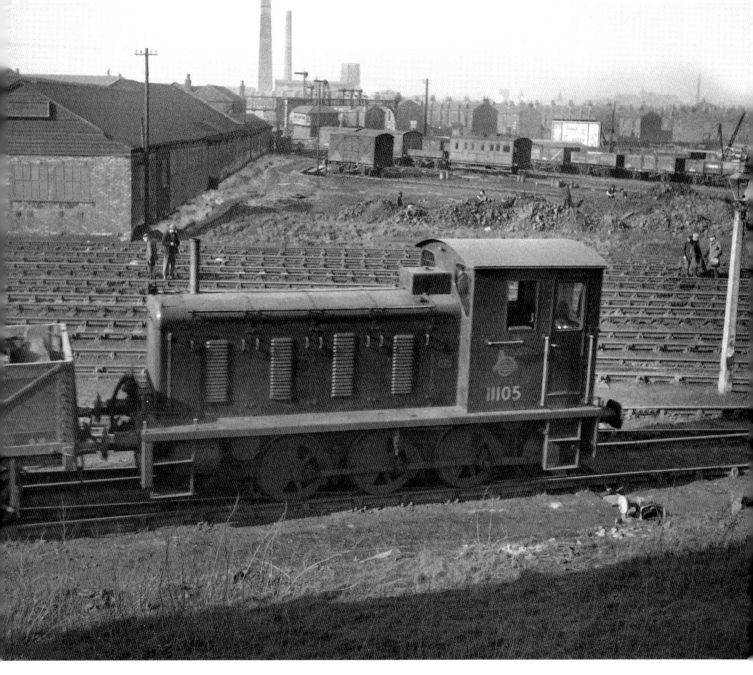

11105 at an earlier – unrecorded – date in black livery and with the retro-fitted box/tank on the bonnet. This timeless scene at West Hartlepool reveals another aspect of the 0-6-0DM from a slightly elevated angle. Whilst we are here, take in the yards, rolling stock, back-to-back terrace housing, semaphore signals, industrial haze, and manual labour. Most, if not quite all of those things have disappeared and belong to an age which now seems so far away. *R.F.Payne.*

(*above*) Spot the deliberate mistake or to be more precise, something of a rarity. LMS/EE Jackshaft 350 h.p. 0-6-0 DE shunter 12016 managed somehow to acquire a 'D' prefix and here at Edge Hill on 24th April 1960 the condensed Grotesque appellation is plain for all to see. Although the locomotive is quite filthy, the number grouping appears to be fairly new. (*below*) The normal number grouping as displayed by 12007 at Speke Junction shed on the same day. Both *J.Archer.*

A rather nice picture of Hunslet 0-6-0DM D2592 at what the notes state to be Darlington shed. We have no date but this particular shunter transferred from Wakefield to West Hartlepool on 8th January 1964. On the left is sister D2588 which arrived at 51C from Ardsley on 25th February 1964; to the right is J94 No.68032 which was condemned at West Hartlepool on 25th May 1964. So, are we at West Hartlepool circa February to May 1964 or at Darlington shed where D2588 and the J94 might meet whilst en route to their respective fates? If the latter, why was D2592 also at 51A? The background offers no clues at all so we must trust the notes and regard the event as an unusual meeting, perhaps. For the record, D2592 left Hartlepool for Haymarket on 9th April 1967 and was withdrawn from that depot on 23rd March 1968. D2588 remained at 51C and was withdrawn on 12th March 1967 being sold for scrap to a Rotherham yard shortly afterwards; the J94 was despatched locally at a Teesside yard. Anyway, it is an excellent picture of a short-lived locomotive which didn't even manage a ten year career before it too was discarded as scrap to a Scottish yard in 1969. *P.J.Robinson.*

Ex-makers splendour at Eastfield shed on a date assumed to be during July 1960, shortly after the North British-built 0-4-0DH had been delivered to 65A. One of twelve such shunters acquired new by Eastfield at that time, it was later joined by ten more of the class at the Glasgow shed. The delivery date for D2764 was actually Friday 8th July, and even then the full regalia of the chevron/wasp/zebra warning stripes at both ends had become the norm, along with the green livery and black frames and wheels; note that a full set of lamp irons have been provided to supplement the electric lighting system. Although fitted with vacuum brakes for train braking, the little shunter has only been equipped with three-link couplings which must have been deemed adequate as these 0-4-0s had a top speed of only 17 m.p.h. – nearly 50% faster than their predecessors. Withdrawn on 3rd February 1968, D2764 entered one of the Scottish scrapyards shortly afterwards for an early demise. *P.J.Robinson.*

Considering that the locomotive works at Stratford handled numerous diesel shunter overhauls every year, it seems to be a bit of a mystery that the two Ruston & Hornsby 0-4-0DM D2957 and D2958, which had been allocated to Stratford depot 30A since January 1957, should go to Doncaster for overhauls. Such was the case in June 1963 when D2957 was photographed at Doncaster shed after attending works there and was waiting for haulage back to the east London depot. Note that the gearbox connection has been removed for long distance transit which would probably have taken place during the week after this Sunday 23rd June image was recorded. Starting life as 11507, this four-coupled shunter was initially allocated to Immingham shed on 6th March 1956 to work the dock lines around the port. In May it was joined at 40B by sister 11508 (D2958). Their time at the Humberside port was not a happy one and at the end of 1956 it was decided to send them both to Stratford for further use in the London docklands. Such was the case until August 1966 when our subject was transferred to Goole, D2958 remaining at Stratford. On 12th March 1967 D2957 was withdrawn whilst its sister lasted until the following January. D2957 was finally hauled away to Rotherham where the Slag Reduction Co. made short work of its 29-ton bulk in the summer of 1967. Purchased by a different yard, D2958 was actually put to work at C.F.Booth's scrapyard, also in Rotherham, where it performed admirably until finally bowing out in 1984. *C.J.B.Sanderson.*

A five thousand horsepower motive power combination passes the junction at Ouston on Saturday 27th July 1964. In actual fact 2,500 h.p. of the total was switched out and the two BR Sulzer Type 2s were doing all the work in rescuing this northbound passenger train of which failed 'Peak' D172 was once in charge. Not far to go now though and D5103, along with D5150 and their brake tender, can get back to normal work or retire to their depot. Branching off to the right is the main line to Consett. *F.W.Hampson.*

An undated view of 'Peak' D166 at Newcastle (Central) after arrival with a Down working in 1962! The scene was captured on film not too long after the big diesel's release to traffic from Derby and subsequent posting to Gateshead depot in early May 1962. This was the first of twenty-eight of the class which settled in at 52A for the duration. Becoming Class 46 under the TOPS scheme, D166 was renumbered to 46029 in October 1973. Transferred to Holbeck in May 1968, D166 soon rejoined the Gateshead crowd and was eventually withdrawn from that depot in January 1983. Here the 'Peak' has just been uncoupled from its train on platform 8, at the east end of the station, and is awaiting a signal which will take it back over the Tyne via the High Level bridge to Gateshead depot. *B.Anderson.*

With its noisy exhausts rendering any casual conversation useless, Finsbury Park 'Deltic' D9007 PINZA stops for a crew change whilst heading a northbound working from King's Cross at Newcastle Central in 1962. Although work-stained, the big diesel still looks magnificent in two-tone green. This is the changeover point where countless numbers of steam locomotives have been taken off or attached to northbound expresses for decades. With the new motive power such operations became unnecessary and only the footplatemen changed over. *B.Anderson.*

Derby based 'Peak' D94 is released from its train at Newcastle Central in 1962 and is making its way to Gateshead depot for refuelling. It was very rare for Derby steam locomotives to work this far north, Leeds or York being the extremity of their travels onto North eastern territory but the diesels knew no boundaries and performed on such through workings on a daily basis, much to the delight of local enthusiasts. *B.Anderson.*

Another look at the east end of platforms 8 and 9 at Newcastle on another unrecorded date but probably circa September 1960, which was not long after EE Type 4 D285 had entered traffic. This illustration would make a superb 'what is being said' caption such as 'I can't go in there, its too clean!' or similar – you can make up your own minds as to what was perhaps said by the footplateman on the platform. D285 was York based at this time according to the shedplate below the number, its first transfer to Gateshead did not take place until 25th March 1967. *Jack Teasdale, Trevor Ermel* collection.

Apologies all around but you will have noticed we are still at Newcastle and at that same changeover point at the east end, between platforms 8 & 9. My reason for loitering here for a few minutes longer was to show you the procedure enacted when a northbound Anglo-Scottish express had to change locomotives. We now see Gateshead's EE type 4 D394 whistling off the centre road and gaining the road for platform 9. Once clear of the points, the big 2,000 h.p. diesel would reverse onto the stock left at the platform – behind the photographer – by a steam locomotive which had quickly uncoupled and retired to Gateshead shed after its journey from the south. Once coupled, D394 would head north after a slick changeover which took not much longer than it did to read this caption – well perhaps a few minutes more. Compare the front ends of the two Vulcan built Type 4s from different periods on opposing pages. Oh! The date – circa July 1962. *B.Anderson.*

D6129 and D6132 stand at the head of an Aberdeen bound express at Glasgow's Buchanan Street station on 4th April 1961. It was on these express services where the Type 2s really began to show their many flaws and because of that, and with no real alternative diesel power available, redundant Gresley A4 Pacifics were drafted in from the ECML. At the time of the photograph, these two were allocated to Eastfield depot having transferred there from Ipswich on 19th June 1960 and 22nd May 1960 respectively. Both were amongst the twenty members of the class which were refurbished and upgraded – from 1000 to 1100 h.p. – in the mid-1960s to become TOPS Class 29 as against the designated Class 21 of their original condition siblings; D6123 was given a Paxman engine rated at 1350 h.p. but became the only one so treated. Our subjects here were rebuilt in April 1967 and March 1966 respectively. Both were withdrawn in October 1971 and cut up at Glasgow works, not far from their birthplace. What of Buchanan Street terminus? Perhaps the least iconic of the four Glasgow termini, this former Caledonian station which opened in November 1849, was closed on 7th November 1966 just five months after the G&SWR terminus at St. Enoch had suffered the same fate. Dieselisation, with the help of Dr Beeching, was taking its toll on BR passenger facilities, everywhere. *D.J.Dippie.*

The photographer managed to record the number of the steam locomotive of this unconventional duo but forget to 'bag' the EE Type 1. The location is Birkett tunnel (462 yards?) on the Settle & Carlisle with a Saturday 15th April 1967 freight working being shared by 'Jubilee' No.45593 and what appears to be a Scottish based diesel with an indented cab side sheet for tablet exchanging equipment. Was the Bo-Bo assisting an ailing steamer or merely hitching a ride? The 'Jubilee' seems to be in a bit of trouble but was nevertheless struggling to do its bit. Did anyone else record this combination? *John Boyes.*

Now here is an Anglo-Scottish express of long standing. The Up *THAMES-CLYDE EXPRESS* is making its way along its usual route on 12th August 1967 with EE Type 4 D357 digging in to the southbound climb. The location is Armathwaite on the S&C main line when things were becoming rather overgrown and dilapidated on that route. How D357 got on the front end of what was usually a 'Peak' working is unknown. Equally mysterious is the fact that this Type 4 was a Haymarket engine and appears to have been 'borrowed' by whichever depot was responsible for providing the motive power. It was going to work as far as Leeds anyway. *John Boyes.*

How to make a Diesel Brake Tender (DBT): Select one standard Gresley designed carriage; take off the upper bodywork and strip right down to the solebars; cut a section of the frame out of the middle of the whole so that you are left with about a foot projecting out from the inner edge of each bogie; weld said frame parts together to create a rigid short vehicle. It is not necessary to remove either the bogies or buffers during any part of the aforementioned operation. Next, construct a secondary frame to attach to the primary frame; place heavy weights (concrete blocks, old rails or pig iron ingot or billets are all useful) and attach by various methods to the primary and secondary frames. Salvage the vacuum brake equipment from the initial strip down and install inside the 'vehicle' where space for such has been left available. Cover the whole thing with some sheet materials – optional – preferably mild steel, cut and shaped to project an element of limo-style streamlining. Finally, paint in diesel fleet green livery and apply the necessary marking for identification, information and advice. Note that only three-link couplings are required, the locomotives own screw coupling would be used normally for attachment. As an interim 'piece of kit' the DBT was a cheap, useful and pretty rugged item of rolling stock which helped BR through the long years of working with tens of thousands of pieces of non-vacuum fitted rolling stock. The DBT added about 35 tons of brake weight to a diesel locomotive making life safer for locomotive crews especially. The bulk of the DBTs were allocated to locomotive depots in the north-east, though they rarely went 'on-shed' and were stabled around the yards. They could also be found on the Western Region and in a few areas of Scotland where their services were required on unfitted mineral workings. This is fairly new No.B964055E which was a recently constructed at York as part of Lot 3448 consisting 62 similar vehicles. The DBT is guiding EE Type 3 D6770 which was equally new to British Railways. Both were allocated to Thornaby depot and the date is circa September 1962. It was usual not to uncouple the tenders between workings so that approximately half of the journeys undertaken by the locomotive would require the DBTs to be propelled. However, it apparently took some getting use to stopping them at signals on the correct side of the track circuitry. *B.Anderson.*

Unusual motive power for the Royal Train perhaps!? On Thursday 19th October 1967, Thornaby EE Type 3 D6763 was in charge of the Royal Train at Billingham and was carrying headcode 3X01 which may well have indicated empty stock. The exact location is unknown to this compiler but it appears to be either a loop or siding alongside the main running lines and the train may well have spent the night at this spot with D6763 providing motive power for any eventuality. The first vehicle seems to be the generator coach followed by staff vehicles whilst those containing the Royal personages – if any were aboard – are beyond. Who was actually on board that day and to what event they were attending is also unknown but perhaps one of our readers can put us in the picture on that one. *John Boyes.*

Please don't write in and accuse us of being Royalists or such like simply because we illustrate the same train from the previous image but from the other end. It is after all a different location and, different motive power. Brush Type 4 D1985 is in charge now and looks like it means business with a headcode more in keeping with its duties – 1X01. Gateshead provided this locomotive and for 52A it is looking remarkably clean considering it had been allocated to the Tyneside depot from new since 17th January 1966, nearly two years (perhaps it had just returned from main works was my first cynical thought). Anyway, 52A had done BR proud. So, where are all the crowds of well wishers? *John Boyes.*

TROUBLE AGAIN

Carrying on our theme of featuring locomotives in trouble, dire or otherwise, we present our first offering in this volume in the shape of BR Sulzer Type 2 D7546 sitting on the ground – half of it anyway. Note the crew, or at least a guard in the near cab. The location is unrecorded but is actually in Wigan. New to Toton (Nottingham Division) on 8th May 1965, the Type 2 transferred to Springs Branch depot on 2nd December 1967, and then to Allerton on 11th May of the following year. Later that year it moved to the newly created Preston Division. The twin chimneys are the main clue and point to Westwood power station which was located just south-west of Wigan (North Western) station – a gas holder belonging to the local gas works is also visible above the grounded section of the diesel. The bogie of D7546 is virtually level with Bridge No.46 (Chapel Lane) at the south end of the WCML station, on the road leading from bay platform No.4. So, the date is possibly between December 1967 and May 1968. Going nowhere, the crew seem to have settled into the newspaper crossword whilst they await assistance. 'Now then, 3 across "This year's National winner?"' *Trevor Ermel.*

This picture of Drewry D2265 at the works crossing at Darlington is undated but in was captured post January 1960 when the adjacent EE Type 4 arrived in the north-east. The vacuum fitted shunter has been involved in an incident which has not only buckled the cab it has also bent the running plate upwards at the back end. The front left buffer appears bent too indicating a rolling stock accident. Without further visual evidence other damage cannot be commented on. What actually caused the damage is unknown, or even when and where the incident occurred. However, the diesel was repaired and sent back to its home shed at Hammerton Street in Bradford. Becoming BR property on 28th December 1957, D2265 was allocated to the Bradford depot and it was still resident when withdrawn in March 1970. Built at the RS&H works in Darlington, it may have been repaired there but more than likely the BR workshops took care of the repair; no doubt components from the contractor's plant found their way to the BR shops once the scale of the damage was revealed. *J.W.Armstrong.*

Ooops! So, who saw what? Brand new, straight out of the box and crunch! D4161 on Darlington shed yard on Monday 30th April 1962 looks a bit shaken after being involved in a shunting incident between main works and the engine shed. Though not severe, the damage is somewhat inconvenient with a few replacement components required; two sandboxes and associated piping, cab steps, and probably a new set of shunters steps too, along with a lick of paint in appropriate places and further sign writing, or were they transfers? Even the works plate appears a bit suspect. The shunter has left his pole on the front steps in either resignation or disbelief. Bound, eventually, for Penzance shed (plenty of scope on that marathon journey to apportion blame somewhere else perhaps?), D4161 arrived in Cornwall at some time during late May, after the necessary return to its birthplace for rectification. *D.J.Dippie.*